I0609982

Frederick A. (Frederick Anthony) Atkins

First Battles and how to fight them

Some friendly Chats with young Men

Frederick A. (Frederick Anthony) Atkins

First Battles and how to fight them
Some friendly Chats with young Men

ISBN/EAN: 9783337135836

Printed in Europe, USA, Canada, Australia, Japan

Cover: Foto ©ninafisch / pixelio.de

More available books at **www.hansebooks.com**

First Battles

AND HOW TO FIGHT THEM.

Some Friendly Chats with Young Men.

BY

FREDERICK A. ATKINS,

AUTHOR OF "MORAL MUSCLE, AND HOW TO USE IT."

"We are like soldiers in a vast, widely-extended battlefield (wrapped
in obscurity) of which we know not the phases, of which we seem utterly
powerless to control the issues; but we are responsible for our own part—
whatever goes on elsewhere, let us not fail in that. The changes of the
world, which men think they are bringing about, are in the hands of
God. With Him, when we have done our duty, let us leave them."—
DEAN CHURCH.

FLEMING H. REVELL COMPANY,

NEW YORK:
30 Union Square: East.

CHICAGO:
148 and 150 Madison Street.

Publishers of Evangelical Literature.

CONTENTS.

INTRODUCTION.

It falls to the lot of most persons to find life a conflict: to some it is a protracted and arduous campaign. This is only to say that, if we would come successfully through it, we must assume the attitude of soldiers, and be well accoutred for the fight. Much as there is in military life which we cannot but deplore, there is no illustration more frequently employed in Scripture to set forth the duties and the character of a Christian; and, however much we may be out of sympathy with the profession, and lament the need for it, it cannot be denied that most of the personal qualities that make a good soldier are just those which go to constitute an exemplary Christian.

A man may be soldierly, no doubt, without possessing even a semblance of piety; but, all other things being equal, the more soldierly he is, the higher will be the type of his religion. If godly men in the army are rare, they are generally exceptionally good! they have the courage of their convictions, and are decidedly aggressive in their piety. Particularly valuable are the qualities referred to in the beginning of life, when temptations are most numerous and powerful. When St.

Paul exhorted his young friend Timothy to be "a good soldier," he gave advice which all young men would do well to lay to heart; and never, perhaps, was it more needful than in an age like this, when the prevalence of luxury and the appetite for pleasure are so apt to take all the *grit* and manliness out of the rising youth of our land. Just as many a raw recruit has joined his country's service, tempted by the seemingly gay and easy life of a soldier, but has found, when called to active duty in the field, that the discipline was very different from what he expected, so it is with thousands of young men in their setting out on life; what promised to be almost a holiday proving a stiff conflict, and demanding a "hardness" they had not calculated upon. The *first battles* are therefore the most trying and crucial.

It is well that this should be understood and prepared for. Many a young man makes a moral collapse, because he did not know of the dangers he had to face, the enemies he had to conquer, and the special qualities he needed to possess; whereas, had he been duly warned and counselled, he might have come through victorious. Those are the best friends of youth who faithfully point out the perils that lie before them, and urge preparation for the fight. No living man better understands how to do this than the author of *First Battles, and How to Fight Them.* I think it was John Bright who happily remarked some years ago, when speaking of a popular nobleman, Lord Roseberry, that he had the face of a boy and the tongue of a sage; and it would be no extravagance to say of our author that his writings combine the vivacity of youth with the mellow wisdom of maturity. He is already favorably known by his little book, *Moral Muscle, and How to Use It*, and has secured a wide influence among the rising generation by his able editorship of THE YOUNG MAN. *First Battles* is an admirable successor to *Moral Muscle*, the title in both cases being singularly felicitous.

One can scarcely fail to be struck with the unusual number of books that have been published within the last few years, specially addressed to young men. The press has clearly been alive to the growing need for this class of literature. At no period of the world, probably, have the claims of young men been so fully recognized, or so much attention been bestowed upon the temptations, difficulties and dangers that specially beset them. This is a hopeful feature of the age; and all the more so because, on the whole, the tone of these endeavors is bracing and invigorating in its character. It is no longer assumed that a young man of undoubted piety must be effeminate in his bearing, morbid and whimsical in his principles, and hostile to every species of physical culture and recreation.

On the other hand, thank God, it is coming to be generally recognized that Christianity aims at saving the whole man, " body, soul, and spirit;" and that genuine religion develops and ennobles all the powers. The author of *First Battles* is a recognized apostle of this doctrine. He is the sworn enemy of cant. He believes that godliness and manliness are close akin. He goes in for a religion that is bright and brotherly, courteous and unselfish, and whose invariable tendency is to elevate and refine, and to turn out true gentlemen. Well does he say, " One of the most remarkable characteristics of gentlemanliness lies in the fact that it is not so very far removed from womanliness. It has a sacred modesty, a tender regard and respect for weakness and loneliness and inferiority, a deep and genuine reverence for the innocence and purity of womanhood. But you say, How about manliness? I reply by asking another question, Do you know what manliness means? It means *virtue*. When Garfield said, ' I shall try and become a man; if I do not succeed in that, I shall be good for nothing,' he did not mean that his ambition was to be merely big and boisterous and robust—he desired to become gentle and strong and good."

The object of this little book, of course, is not to teach theology, but there is not a sentence in it that is not in harmony with healthy evangelical teaching. The writer is not forgetful of the Cross, with its wondrous mystery and its matchless power; but his special aim is to present to young men the living Christ, as at once the brightest example and the truest Friend. Leaving Christian doctrine to be handled by others, he shows what Christian practice is; and to all who, under cover of religion, allow in themselves anything that is false or cowardly or mean, he administers vigorous and merited castigation. The perusal of these pages cannot but be useful to all who are just entering on life's first battles; here they will find the wise counsels and cheering words they need. For young men who are leaving school and home, and going forth to push their own way in the world, a more suitable gift could hardly be selected than *First Battles, and How to Fight Them.*

J. THAIN DAVIDSON.

First Battles,

AND HOW TO FIGHT THEM.

I.

MONEY AND MORALS.

"*When a man dies, they who survive him ask what property he has left behind him. The angel who bends over the dying man asks what good deeds he has sent before him.*"—THE KORAN.

"*It is physically impossible for a well-educated, intellectual, or brave man to make money the chief object of his thoughts.*"—RUSKIN.

IT seems a strange combination! Is there any connection between money and morals? If there is it is the connection which exists between the neck of the criminal and the axe of the executioner— a connection that is, as a rule, hopelessly and absolutely fatal. The reckless greed of gain has driven more men away from Jesus Christ than any other passion. "Very sorrowful . . . for he was

5

very rich." That is a miniature portrait
of a young man who once came to Christ,
and it tells the story of many a prosperous
but dissatisfied man to-day. Have you
ever known any man who received the
slightest benefit of a high and noble kind
from money? Has it ever made a man
good? Has it ever increased his gener-
osity, broadened his sympathies, or roused
in him a longing after righteousness?
Never! It adds to your creature com-
forts, ministers to your merely sensuous
enjoyment; if you possess brains it enables you to encourage art and science,
and if you are a practical Christian it
places in your hand the wherewithal to
succor the suffering and relieve the dis-
tressed. But in itself money has never
made any man happy or healthy or holy.
On the contrary, it has dimmed the love,
wrecked the peace, and spoilt the characters of countless thousands. One of the
ablest preachers of the day, speaking re-

cently, said that " nothing but the mercy of God prevented money from doing harm wherever it went."

Don't you think it is a very impressive and significant fact that the most heartless and contemptible act of treachery ever committed—an act which has excited the horror and disgust of all the ages—should have been due to the selfish desire of a miserable and covetous man to secure thirty pieces of silver? Judas Iscariot was not a degraded profligate—he was a disciple, with a character, no doubt, of the utmost decency and respectability. He may have been alluded to, for all we know, as a shrewd, practical, hard-headed man of business. But it was that little bag of money which led to his sin, his suicide, and his destruction. His love of gain was greater than his love for his Lord.

And this is just where the danger exists. Young men will exclaim, " Surely

it is not wrong to wish to make money?"
Certainly not, if you are careful that when
you have *made* the money it does not *mar*
you. Riches are like a rose in a man's
hand; if he holds it gently it will preserve
its beauty of shape and fragrance of smell,
but if he handles it tightly he will crush
and destroy it. Make your pile of money
if you will—work on with earnestness, industry, and persistence, and may large
success attend all your endeavors. But
bear with this brotherly warning. Hold
the riches lightly—let them flow out free-
ly in wise benevolence, use them liberally
for the highest ends, and you will have
done well. But hug your wealth, set your
heart on it, let the miserly and covetous
spirit paralyze your very soul, and life
will become a hideous nightmare, a foul
sepulchre, a long spell of hopeless servitude.

Do you doubt this? Then listen to the
testimony of a man who made money

with great rapidity and got rid of it with equal celerity. "I have never seen the use of hoarding money," said George Moore; "we may gather riches, but can never know who is to spend them. God preserve me against the sin of covetousness. It is a curse that eats out the heart and dries up the soul of a man." Have we not all seen the man who is rich and wretched? He has given up his life to the pursuit of wealth, and in so doing the man has been utterly lost in the machine. When his bank-book bulges out with untold riches, he finds that it is impossible to enjoy them. He has cultivated no lofty tastes, formed no healthy habits, indulged in no Christly beneficence, and so the money is nothing but an intolerable burden, and all he can do is to go on raking, and reckoning, and grinding, and fighting for gold that he does not want, and which he does not know how to use when it is acquired.

Beware of this reckless and ruinous ambition for wealth. Remember the words of Goethe—

> Men may bear much from harsh severity,
> But not a long run of unmixed prosperity!

Riches are like thorns—touch them tenderly and lightly and they are harmless; rest on them and they will cut and rend and pierce you. Therefore do not allow your mind to be muddled and your life to be unsettled by a vain desire for a big bank balance. "A restlessness in men's minds," says Sir William Temple, "to be something they are not, and to have something they have not, is the root of all immorality." That is profoundly and terribly true. We forget that a good farthing is better than a bad sovereign, and that it is far more manly to do the best we can with our own feathers than to strut in borrowed plumes. Why should we be so anxious for the gilded shams and sparkling mockeries of the world? Is a man's heart more restful because his head is adorned with a coronet? Does his life gain in buoyancy because he keeps more horses than he can ride? What nonsense it all is! Instead of spoiling your life by any mad ambition for personal aggrandizement, do the present duty manfully and well. After all *that* is the surest road to prosperity. And if you have sufficient grit in you to stand the overwhelming temptations of riches, they *may* be bestowed on you one of these days, and then you will wonder how you could ever have wasted a single moment in longing for so fleeting and superficial a possession. But never allow the devil to make you morbidly discontented with your environment. If he once does that, he can work your ruin without much further trouble. "You were meant," he will say, "for something better than this monotonous toil; get gold and plenty of it, put on fine airs, and help to swell the mob of fashionable

pleasure-seekers; live for sensual delights, smother your conscience with
bank-notes, and laugh at the puritanical
ravings of modern faddists and philan-
thropic cranks." The man who is
caught by this temptation seldom escapes.
He gambles and plunges furiously, and
tries to get rich by rapid and unrighteous
means. He becomes selfish and cynical
and dishonest, winks at falsehood, laughs
at license, is unscrupulous in his passion for
wealth and position, and, almost without
knowing it, the poor fellow has sunk into
the uttermost depths of cowardice and
vice. There is, however, an ambition
which is noble and commendable, but it
is ruled by love, guarded by honesty, and
sanctified by a generous goodwill towards
men. The best ambition is the ambition
to be good and brave and true. Let us
not be at the beck and call of every passing fancy. Let us earnestly and cour-
ageously perform the task intrusted to us,

however lowly it may be, and however inadequate its reward. To us it may seem the dreariest drudgery, but when we do it well and cheerfully for Christ's sake, even drudgery becomes divine.

Many years ago Charles Kingsley, as "Parson Lot," inaugurated a valiant crusade against the mammon worship of his day. Of course he met with the bitter and virulent hostility of all who loved money more than justice and brotherly love. But he earned an undying reputation as the friend and champion of humanity. We want another "Parson Lot" in these days to teach us that money is not a thing to be played with at the will of its possessor. Nothing will help so much to solve certain modern problems as the dissemination of Bible teaching regarding money. The idea of the Bible is distinctly that of stewardship. The money you put away in the bank is, in a limited and mechanical sense, your own property.

But looked at from the higher and more Christian standpoint, it is not yours at all. It is given to you as a *trust*, not as a possession. If that great and unassailable principle could prevail in the minds and hearts of men, gambling would be annihilated once and for all. Because the old stock argument in favor of betting—it generally comes from flabby, unhealthy young men of dissipated life and restricted intellect—is this: "Oh, but you know, old fellow, a man can do as he likes with his own money." Certainly; I grant that entirely. But the fact is that the money is not yours. God has placed it in your hands for fifty or sixty years, and there will come a day of reckoning when He will want to know what good you have accomplished, what poverty you have relieved and what evil you have destroyed by the powerful and influential gift which He intrusted in your keeping. One hardly likes to think what the result will be when you have to confess that you tossed the gold to the devil—that you flung it away at poker or that you handed it to some rascally poolseller.

It is impossible to write of money and morals without protesting against the biggest curse of modern times. Nothing is more calculated to turn the smiling optimist into a despairing pessimist than the incalculable ruin which is being wrought every day by betting and gambling. This is undoubtedly the most serious and difficult problem with which Christian reformers have to grapple. So far we have scarcely touched it. There have been long and wordy discussions, a great deal of purposeless chatter has been poured forth in speeches and leading articles, and still we seem to make no progress—we are engaged in the useless occupation of beating the air. Convocation will not untie the knot; the newspaper is impotent simply because it is implicated ;

and Christian men are too apt to trust to silvery rhetoric rather than to stringent reform.

The fact is, that nothing very helpful will be done until we clear our minds of cant. The practical common-sense of solemn dignitaries who fervently denounce betting and then sit down to play whist for dime points is somewhat difficult to detect. The wisdom of arresting one gambler and asking another to open a church bazaar is scarcely perceptible to the man in the street. Betting is fashionable; the gambler is a respected, or at least a tolerated, individual, and even the great mass of Christian men and women have not yet had their eyes opened to the awful havoc caused by this passionate lust for gain. When they see how it robs men of character, health, and friends; when they realize that horse-racing has more votaries than any religion; then, I believe, they will rise up and denounce it fearlessly. The literature of the turf is enormous in extent and world-wide in influence. It provides a risky excitement for the rich and a hideous fever for the poor. It shows men how to get hold of their neighbors' property without giving any honest equivalent, which means, in plain English, that it makes men thieves.

It is simply alarming to contemplate the extent to which the deadly contagion is spreading through the country. Boys bet; young men neglect the beauties of literature for the "tips" of sporting papers ; and scarcely an office is without its sweep-stake on the Derby or the boat-race. This vice controls its victims with a fascination which is absolutely devilish, and the unutterable ruin which it inevitably works is almost heartbreaking. I therefore call upon every earnest, manly, Christian fellow to do all he can to stamp out this degrading and unchivalrous

habit. For this two reasons are sufficient : — (1) It must be wrong to accept
money for which you have given nothing
in return; and (2) it is the very essence
of selfishness to use, as Kingsley says,
" what you fancy your superior knowledge of a horse's merits to your neighbor's harm." " Work faithfully," says
Mr. Ruskin, " and you will put yourself
in possession of a glorious and enlarging
happiness ; not such as can be won by
the speed of a horse or marred by the
obliquity of a ball."

All thoughtful and observant men must
admit that materialism is the dominant
peril of our age. As young men. therefore, we must be on our guard. Wealth
is a useful servant when guarded by charity and wisdom, but it is a tyrannical master, and holds its subjects in galling and
miserable servitude. Christ never thought
much of money. The most hopeless and
melancholy characters He ever drew

were rich men. His Gospel teaches us
that character is more than circumstances
—a clean heart better than a big check-
book. Bacon has called riches "the baggage of virtue." "As baggage is to an
army," he says, "so is riches to virtue; it
cannot be spared or left behind, but it
hindereth the march. Of great riches
there is no real use, except it be in the
distribution; the rest is but conceit." I
have heard of a very wealthy merchant,
who, attending church one night, was
greatly impressed by the words of Christ,
"A rich man shall hardly enter into the
kingdom of heaven." They lingered in
his memory, and for years his rest was
broken and his peace disturbed by this
discomforting thought, "*Shall hardly
enter.*" Let us frankly confess then that
if we have given our hearts over to mammon worship, we have, to say the least of
it, made a tremendous mistake. The
millionaire is not always the successful

man.   The richest merchant in the city
may in reality be poorer than his meanest
servant.   For all the money on earth
cannot compensate for a starved soul, a
narrow mind, a limited outlook, and a life
that confers no blessing on humanity.
"Chinese" Gordon was comparatively
poor, but he achieved what was better
than all the fortunes of all the world's
millionaires put together—a Christ-like
character and a noble life-work. Who
would not infinitely prefer to be Gordon
with empty pockets than the richest gambler in the land?

Over the triple doorways of the cathedral of Milan there are three inscriptions
spanning the splendid arches.   Over one
is carved a wreath of roses with the
legend, "All that which pleases is but for
a moment." Over the other is sculptured
a cross accompanied by the words, "All
that which troubles is but for a moment."
But on the great central entrance to the

main aisle is the inscription, "That only is important which is eternal." The lesson is obvious. It teaches us that morals are of more account than money, and that if we are wise we shall care less and less for the passing pageants of the hour, for the gratification of our frivolous fancies, and for the attainment of our worldly ambitions. We shall live for the heavenly, for the eternal, for the service of the strong and tender Christ, whose "well done" is more to be desired than all the plaudits of the universe.

II.

WHAT IS A GENTLEMAN?

And thus he bore without abuse
The grand old name of gentleman,
Defamed by every charlatan,
And soiled with all ignoble use.
—TENNYSON.

NEVER imagine that the swaggering brag-gart can move the world—he is as feeble as he is loud. Jesus Christ was the strong-est man who ever lived—and the gentlest. He would not have hurt the feelings of a child, and yet He could conquer hell. "He opened His mouth and taught them, saying, *Blessed* . . ." That was the keynote of His life. He was always blessing somebody—healing the sick, comforting the sad, cheering the weary, raising the dead; His life was one long series of kindly, brotherly actions. And yet, how He could burn with moral indig-nation! The same Christ who was ten-

(22)

der and gentle and forgiving to the sinners who were tired of the dreary heartache of their useless lives, and longed to be better and do better, could denounce the hypocrites of His day as "a generation of vipers." We must rid ourselves of the popular delusion that tenderness denotes weakness. It doesn't. Bullies are weak —gentlemen are strong. The braggart is impotent; the empty noise of his braying is quickly exhausted, and then he is used up and has nothing to go on with. The man who endures and overcomes is the man who follows Christ in His sweet reasonableness of temper and thought and action.

What is a gentleman? First of all, let me tell you what he is *not*. He is not that well-known youth, with vacant, lamb-like expression, gorgeous necktie of many colors, immense cuffs, large trousers, tiny shoes, and a buttonhole of huge dimensions. He is not the kind of young man whom Charlotte Bronte once described as "pretty-looking and pretty-behaved, apparently constructed without a backbone, by which I don't allude to his corporal spine, which is all right enough, but to his character." We all know this nerveless automaton. He is destitute of one throbbing impulse or lofty ideal. Kingdoms might crash, empires might totter and fall—he soars above such trifles, and views them with stately unconcern. The only matters which trouble him are the straightness of his necktie, the smoothness of his hair, and the whiteness of his cuffs. One day somebody suggests that lawn tennis is a nice, gentle game, and this amiable youth becomes quite interested. Of course he "hasn't an idea how to play," but he knocks the balls about for a quarter of an hour, and is ill with exhaustion for a week afterwards. In company he is silent, hoping, perhaps, that his ravishing beauty may make up for his helpless taciturnity.   He is too modest to sing a song, too lazy to learn an instrument, too dignified to ride a bicycle, too stiff to run a race, too noble to stoop to the clamor of debate or the jealousies of journalism, and much too prudent to venture on any more dogmatic assertion than "Nith day after the wain."   The inconvenient question was asked one day concerning a man of this caliber, "What can he do?"   Well, truth to tell, he can look ladylike, behave beautifully, curl his hair to perfection, and pose for a photograph —rare accomplishments, which, in a more advanced age, might perhaps win for him respect and admiration.   Let us do him justice, however; he is vain but not vicious, puny but not prodigal, languid but never licentious, though certain cynics have suggested that he is mildly respectable only because he lacks the pluck to be madly riotous.   It is an old saying and a true one that " Fine feathers do not make fine birds." A decorated donkey is a donkey still. The slaves of nineteenth century masherdom may be exquisitely beautiful, but they are not gentlemen in the noblest sense of the word.

No ; ladylikeness of exterior and a sort of " got - up - regardless - of - expense " appearance are not the outward and visible signs of gentlemanliness. Some of the roughest and most erratic men possess the truest hearts and the tenderest spirits. I shall always feel intensely grateful that the blind and blundering Peter was one of the disciples, for it shows that Jesus Christ can sympathize with men who are recklessly enthusiastic. Some of the most useful, genial, and delightful men I have ever met have been impetuous Peters— true and honest disciples, but afflicted with the unhappy knack of occasionally doing the right thing in the wrong way. They seem to possess every other virtue except caution and prudence. And yet what a gentleman this erratic kind of fellow sometimes is! How sunny his smile, how loving his heart, how honest his voice, how firm the grip of his hand, and, alas! how unreliable his promises! Write him a long and important letter, and insist in several postscripts on an immediate reply. You may, by means of unusually favorable circumstances or a wet day, receive an answer within a week; but it is more likely that after many days he will be surprised by finding your letter in an odd corner, and write off an apologetic but almost illegible postcard. We all know the man, nimble-minded, keen-witted, and apparently reckless, always eager to listen to a new story, always ready with a good yarn in return. He has boundless energy, never-failing vivacity, and a heart that overflows with love. There is no game or recreation that he does not dabble in. He can ride any kind of cycle, he revels in cricket,

and he can swim like a duck. But he
flies from one to the other with the most
delightful inconsistency, one day perspir-
ing at lawn tennis, a week later rowing
as if for dear life, and anon ready to enter
into an ardent dispute with any man who
dares to assert that gymnastics do not form
the best exercise in the world. In one
word, he is a *rocket*—he may go up, he
may splutter and fall. If he does go up
there is sure to be a brilliant display, for
his ability is undeniable, and his career is
only hindered from being a conspicuous
success by his erratic and disorderly
methods. But look at him and tell me
if he is not a gentleman. See how he
dries the falling tear ; observe how read-
ily he bears the bitterest inconvenience
in order to do a service for a man who is
"down"; notice how he stints himselt
that he may help any prodigal who hap-
pens to be "hard up" ; see how the tiny
children love this great-hearted, merry,

boyish fellow, climbing all over him, caressing his rough face, and pulling his grizzly beard. Yes, this man knows something of the gentlemanly Carpenter of Nazareth, or he could not be so refreshingly frank, so transparently sincere, so sublimely unselfish. After all, I would rather have the rugged warmth of a firework than the prim and pompous frigidity of an iceberg.

But let us come to close quarters, and inquire into some of the indispensable characteristics of a gentleman. In the first place, he is brimming over with *brotherliness.* Not only is this the first indication of gentlemanliness—it is the very essence and heart of true Christianity. The Apostle John evidently thought so, for he said, in his frank, straightforward way, that "If a man say, I love God, and hateth his brother, he is a liar"; and again, "Let us love one another, for love is of God; and every one that loveth

is born of God and knoweth God "; and
then, in a burst of indignation, he de-
clares that the man who hates his brother
is a murderer. I firmly believe that the
crowning necessity of the Church to-day is
not an austere and unbending Puritanism,
but a large-hearted, cheerful spirit of
Christian brotherliness. While we have
been wasting our strength in drawing up
resolutions, arranging our formulas, and
throttling enthusiasm with red tape, the
devil has been winning hosts of adherents
by means of cheerful resorts, bright music,
and good fellowship. The shallow critic
cannot save the world—even the skillful
theologian cannot do it. What we want
is *sympathy.* There are men who have
fallen in the tragedy of life, and, bleeding
and forlorn, they need the hearty hand-
grasp, the friendly help of brotherly men.
We must cast away our supercilious self-
conceit and our chilling cynicism. We
must get hold of those who have been over-

come of evil, and cheer them with words
of hope, and encourage them to begin a
better life. We must treat with infinite
tenderness bewildered, misguided, unhappy souls who have blundered and
fallen, and are gradually sinking into
despair. Such men will be repulsed by a
tract, they will resent an arrogant inquisi-
tion into their intellectual eccentricities.
But we may *love* them to Christ. We may
gently succor them from their evil selves
and show them the noble character,
the mysterious self-sacrifice, and the
resistless power of Him who was the
Friend and Savior of thieves and harlots.
All brotherliness must begin at the Cross.
Inspired by the supreme revelation of the
Father's love, we shall lose our unworthy
pride, our reckless ambition, and our false
notions of respectability, and learn the first
lesson of gentlemanliness, which is to love
our brother even as Christ has loved us.

Then you will always notice that a gen-

tleman possesses a dexterous and most delightful tact.   I think it was Dr. Culross
who, at a gathering of young men, gave
an admirable example of this quality.
He said that at a certain breakfast a guest
upset a cup, and its contents soiled
the cloth.   A neighbor quietly placed a
vase of flowers over the stain, and thus
hid the blot with beauty.   Another story
occurs to me about General Grant, who
avoided taking Lee's presentation sword
at the capitulation without either " clumsy
bluntness or caddish showiness," simply
by adding this to the terms, " All officers
to retain their side-arms."   A third example is given by Mr. R. L. Stevenson,
who reminds us of how Wellington,
meeting Marmont years after Salamanca,
was asked by the agreeable marshal his
opinion of the battle.   "I early per-
ceived," was his gentle reply, " that your
excellency had been wounded."   I mention these incidents to explain what I

mean by a " dexterous tact"—a considera-
tion for the feelings of others, a desire to
put people at their ease, and to make the
best of a trying situation. After all, this
is summed up in the Christian law of
bearing one another's burdens, and of
doing to others as we would others should
do to us.

But if we imitate the gentlemanliness
of Jesus we shall go further, we shall look
for the good in men, we shall try to ignore their weaknesses, and our judgments
will be very kind. We must remember
that no man is utterly and irretrievably
bad. We all have a good side to our character—a Dr. Jekyll, who is generous and
charitable and upright. And alas! what
life is not embittered and hampered by a
ghostly Mr. Hyde, black with iniquity,
terrible with hatred, scorched with hell!
Hercules, the strong man, had a robe
sent to him poisoned with blood. He
put it on, and as soon as it became warm

the poison entered his flesh; he could not tear it from him, and he died, strong man as he was. The evil spirit is part of us, it destroys our rest, it assails us at our weakest points, and when we would do good there is the desperate and deadly temptation to be reckoned with, and sometimes we are swept along before the withering blast of our unrestrained passions. Life is a mixed quantity. We are bad for a time, then we rise up and declare that we will be Christ's men. We pray with eager desire and intense earnestness, and immediately afterwards give both hands to the devil. One day we are cursed with hideous and soul-haunting thoughts, and the very next day blessed with all the calm of heaven's peace. Our life is a maze, a tangled mystery, a grim tragedy. The great lesson to be learnt from this duality of purpose is that no character is altogether bad. The worst part of a man's nature may have caught our attention, and we instantly condemn him as a most hopeless and degraded sinner. What blind injustice! He may all the time be fighting a winning battle with a thousand temptations of which we know nothing. So we must cultivate a gentlemanly kindness in our criticisms, knowing that we shall often experience the pain of defeat ere we know the glory of ultimate victory.

Among other unmistakable indications of true gentlemanliness are chivalry and unselfishness. He is no gentleman, but the meanest and most contemptible of creatures, who is unclean in thought and unchaste in life. One of the most remarkable characteristics of gentlemanliness lies in the fact that it is not so very far removed from womanliness. It has a sacred modesty, a tender regard and respect for weakness and loneliness and inferiority, a deep and genuine reverence for the innocence and purity of woman-

hood. But, you say, how about manliness? I reply by asking another question, Do you know what manliness
means? It signifies *virtue*. When
Garfield said, " I shall try and become a
man ; if I do not succeed in that I shall
be good for nothing," he did not mean
that his ambition was to be merely big
and boisterous and robust, he desired to
become gentle and strong and good.
Vice is no mark of cleverness or manliness. It is a shameful, devilish thing that
scars the soul, wounds the heart, rends
the whole life asunder, and turns the future into darkness.

There is one other mark of the highest
Christian gentlemanliness—it absolutely
prohibits sickening personalities in conversation. "There are times," says Dr.
John Hall, "when we are compelled to
say, ' I do not think Bouncer is a true and
honest man.' But where there is no
need to express an opinion, let poor

Bouncer swagger away. Others will take his measure no doubt, and save you the trouble of analyzing him and instructing them." The gentlemanly thing to do is to dwell as much as possible on the best side of human nature. Healthy men will not wish to dine at a dissecting table. Instead of retailing petty gossip about people, and criticising small mistakes, and exaggerating trifling defects, rise higher, speak of nobler things, manlier thoughts, loftier objects, and try and keep the atmosphere pure and fragrant with charity and brotherly love. Perhaps it has not occurred to you that to ridicule or slander an absent man is the most vulgar and cowardly thing you can do. The Apostle has told us that "the tongue is a fire," and we know it is so. Nothing stabs so deep as slanderous and bitter words. Avoid suspicion, resentment, subtle and base insinuations, and scorn to indulge in unwholesome gossip ;

for, as Cardinal Newman wisely said, the true gentleman " has no ears for slander, never takes an unfair advantage, and interprets everything for the best."

III.

HOW TO BE INSIGNIFICANT.

Honor and shame from no condition rise ;
Act well your part, there all the honor lies.—POPE.

" *To be at work, to do things for the world, to turn the*
currents of the things about us at our will, to make
our existence a positive element, even though it be no
bigger than a grain of sand, in this great system
where we live,—that is a new joy of which the idle
man knows no more than the mole knows of the
sunshine, or the serpent of the eagle's triumphant
flight into the upper air. The man who knows indeed
what it is to act, to work, cries out, ' This, this alone is
to live !' "—PHILLIPS BROOKS.

THE world is full of insignicant people. They are born, they go to school,
they work, they eat, they sleep, they
talk—rather frivolously, they live—very
aimlessly, and one day they die, and the
world is not much the poorer because of
their disappearance. A few men struggle to the front, rise beyond the humdrum
level of the crowd, and make their voices
heard above the common clamor. But

as for the rest, they are insignificant.
Why?   Because it is the easiest thing in
the world.

Probably the surest way to be insignifi-
çant is to inherit wealth.   It is generally
the greatest possible curse for a man to
begin life in opulence.   It ties his hands,
lowers his ambition, and narrows his sympathies.   He is fettered by fashion, and
bound tightly by the conventional preju-
dices of society.   He will not succeed in
journalism, for he cannot bend his back
to begin with the daily drudgery.   He
will hardly consent to soil his hands in
trade ; and as for science and art, why
should he endure the long toil and severe
training of the student when he can oc-
cupy the pleasurable position of the pa-
tron ?   Except in a few remarkable cases,
the young man who enters on life's
tragedy to the music of jingling gold
plays an insignificant part, far from
danger, and therefore far from honor.

My brother, be extremely thankful if you are thrown entirely on your own resources. Many of the men who have won the highest success in commerce and science and art, many of the boldest reformers, most brilliant writers, and most forceful orators, have been men who commenced life without a penny in their pockets. One of the best men I have ever known once thoughtlessly sneered at a young journalist because he lacked the supposed advantage of a college education. He did not know that the successful journalists in the city of London this day who can put B. A. after their names can be comfortably counted on the fingers of one hand. The smartest journalist in that city to-day had no schooling after he reached twelve years of age, except what he gained by his own unaided efforts. It may seem the strangest paradox, but it is nevertheless a simple undeniable fact, that poverty is often one of the greatest blessings a man can have in beginning his career. It nerves him for the battle, it hinders self-indulgence, and it is a sure preventive of laziness.

Another certain method of acquiring insignificance is a love of ease. "Anything for a quiet life" is the motto which has ruined the prospects of thousands. The man who is content to *exist*—the man who says that work is an excellent thing, and he would rather enjoy a short spell of it, but he feels that " to work between meals is not good for the digestion"—that man will always be miserably small and contemptibly insignificant. You have got to *climb* the ladder of life— there is no elevator to take you up. There are prizes to be had, but you must *win* them—they will not drop into your hands. Do you wish to avoid insignificance and rise to some nobler height of work and character and attainment ?   Then you must be ready not only to take opportunities, but to make them. You must be trenuous in effort, dogged in persever-ance, indomitable in courage, and cheer-ful and alert in mind. When Cromwell was asked to postpone an enterprise and "wait till the iron was hot," he bravely replied that he would *make* the iron hot by striking it. That is the dauntless spirit we want to-day—the spirit which laughs at difficulty, and is not to be turned aside from its ambition by all the amiable warnings of prudence or timidity. There is one hymn which is sometimes sung at revival meetings—we do not hear it so often now. It begins—

Oh, to be nothing, nothing.

Now if that is your ambition, you can easily gratify it. Nothingness is soon achieved. But surely no young man with a healthy mind and a Christ-like spirit will be deceived by this hideous mockery and caricature of true humility. To want to be nothing is an insult to the God who made you. Was it worth while bringing you into the world to whine and cant about being nothing? Rouse yourself and think! God has surrounded you with a wealth of privileges and an infinitude of priceless blessings. You inherit all the wisdom and genius and benevolence of the ages—riches that are vast, golden, immortal. You are placed within reach of the noblest possibilities; you have all the help and advantage which come of dwelling in a Christian and civilized land; you live in an age when the zeal and ardor and strength of young men are greatly in demand, and when the opportunities for usefulness are singularly favorable; and yet in the meanest, laziest, most spiritless fashion you ask to be " nothing, nothing." Give up, once for all, this cowardly and characterless whimpering. Be something. Be a *man!*

Shake off your dull sloth and rise to a nobler life. Do you murmur about the fierce and relentless competition? There is no competition *at the top.* The crowd is at the bottom; but look ahead, battle forward, fight your way against every difficulty, valiantly overcome every obstacle, and by the time you have climbed half-way to success you will find that the throng which once pressed around you begins to thin and disappear. And when by skill and industry, faith and fortitude, pluck and perseverence, you have attained the height you set your young heart on reaching, you will discover that there is no competition there—you will then be able to dictate your own terms, and claim the adequate reward of honest, skillful, earnest work.

Yet another most fruitful cause of insignificance is what I should call "time-frittering." Some months ago several of the most prominent ministers in New

York were persuaded to give their views on "The Best Use of Leisure," for the guidance of young men. I am not sure that there is any topic of much greater importance than this, for you can generally tell the character of a man with almost infallible accuracy, by the way in which he uses his leisure hours. Time-frittering is undoubtedly the besetting sin of the young men of to-day. Thousands of fellows turn with horror from actual dissipation. But their virtue is of a negative and therefore of a very worthless kind. They abstain from evil, but they never do any good. The worst and most costly extravagance of which you can be guilty is to throw away your evenings. They are golden opportunities for which you are responsible, and of which you should make the best and highest use. One of the most popular of our writers and orators was once asked how he managed to get through such a prodigious amount of work. "Simply by organizing my time," he replied. It is by this invaluable habit of organizing your leisure hours that you will be able to " wrestle from life its uses and gather from life its beauty." It is wonderful what may be accomplished by devoting the evenings to some useful study or helpful recreation. Earnest and persistent students have learnt several languages in the odd hours of a busy career. Never be afraid of giving up one or two nights a week to your books. " Knowledge is power " all the world over, and what you learn will be sure to come in useful one day. It is an old saying, but I may repeat it with advantage, that " Time-wasting in youth is one of the mistakes which are beyond correction."

Let me mention two more paths to insignificance. One is the loss of a good name. A blasted reputation will carry you into nothingness at express speed. Lose your character, and men will drop

you with stinging promptitude, and you
will sink into the lowest depths of insignificance.   Scarcely anybody will want
to know you—nobody will employ you,
and only a few Christ-like souls will be
ready to lend you a helping hand.   We
are too apt to read the Bible nowadays
as if it were an old-world story, which
has no bearing on the practical matters
of everyday business.   But has it never
struck you that " a good name is rather
to be chosen than great riches," even as
a worldly investment?   Punctuality, con-
centration of effort, ceaseless energy, and
many other qualifications, will help a
man forward ; but, possessing all these,
he may yet be a miserable failure
if he has not a good name.   Character
stands for a good deal, even in these days
of fraud and deceit.   A band of thieves
will want an honest treasurer, and men
who are themselves full of trickery will
appreciate a sturdy, honest character in

others. The young man whose word cannot be relied upon, whose honesty is not beyond suspicion, and whose personal life is not clean, will search in vain for a position in the business world to-day. Be careful that you never lose your good name. It may take you ten or twenty years to gain a high and spotless reputation, but you can easily destroy it in ten minutes ; and a man who has once proved himself unworthy to be trusted will find it an almost helpless task to win back confidence and regard. He may even possess influence, and family position, and hosts of friends ; but the way upward will be hard and thorny, because he once surrendered his reputation. Be on your guard, be watchful and vigilant ; let him that thinketh he standeth take heed lest he fall. Count your good name as a possession above price, and by the strong help of your Father God, never permit it to soiled or sullied. Honesty is better than brilliance ; purity and uprightness are greater than dash and cleverness.

I must refer to one other way in which you may become insignificant—it is by turning your back on God. Do that, and although you are decorated with all the tinsel honors of the world, your selfish, shrivelled, narrow little soul will be a daily torment to you. The foundation of all true success is an unswerving fidelity to the highest religious principle. I like to think of George Moore—the uncouth country boy — going to London with little education, less money, and no introduction ; indeed, with nothing but a brave heart and a fervent trust in his God. At first he met with the keenest disappointments, but his manly courage never gave way. He was determined not to sink into nothingness and insignificance. He pushed, and prayed, and persevered, and the opening soon came, as it always does to vigorous and high-minded fellows, and after some years George Moore, the merchant prince, was giving away money at the rate of $80,000 a year. He would not have achieved this if he had been a thoughtless, shiftless, lounging ne'er-do-well. The great secret of his wonderful success was his simple unaffected piety. Men trusted him implicitly because of his genuine godliness. Brothers, never imagine for a moment that Christianity is a vapid, fastidious, sentimental thing. The truest heroes have been the truest Christians. Think of Paul and Luther, and Havelock and Gordon, General Lee and strong, noble, manly souls, unfettered by guile or meanness, unfaltering in their transparent sincerity of character, and in their unbending loyalty to truth. Believe me, nothing will do so much to save a man from insignificance as a chivalrous, upright character, and a simple, stalwart faith in God.

Go forth 'mong men, not mailed in scorn,
But in the armor of a pure intent ;
Great duties are before you, and great aims,
And whether crowned or crownless when you fall,
It matters not, so be God's work is done.

IV.

THE PHILOSOPHY OF PLEASURE.

" We must deal with pleasures as we do with honey, only touch them with the tip of the finger, and not with the whole hand, for fear of surfeit."—VENERABLE BEDE.

" They came to a delicate plain called Ease, where they went with much content, but that plain was but narrow, so they were quickly got over it."—PILGRIM'S PROGRESS.

PLEASURE is the most uncertain thing in the world. That which gives one man a glow of genuine happiness is to another man nothing but unutterable weariness. And more remarkable still, that which bores a man at one time will delight him at another. But the strangest characteristic of pleasure is this : that it is not to be bought with money, or acquired by effort, or secured by influence. " Fly pleasure," says Shakespeare, " and it will follow thee." And we may well add, " Pursue it, and it will utterly fade away." Pleas-

ures are transitory, mysterious, and, to a
large extent, dangerous. They are dangerous in this sense, that they need to be
governed, restrained, and limited by wisdom, by piety, and by Christian sagacity.

The transient and evanescent nature
of pleasure is seen in the fact that half
the enjoyment of life is in anticipation.
How the keen, shrewd man of business
revels in his work! To him it is full of
romance, interest, and excitement. He
has made up his mind to succeed, to attain a high reputation, to build up a great
career, and to earn a fortune. Now look
ahead. He has completed his task and
retired from work. All his desires are
more than fulfilled, and life would seem
to be a garden of beauty and comfort and
unsullied joy. That is where you are
mistaken. He is miserable. He has .
acquired a huge fortune, but his happiest
days were spent in making it; and he
would give a good deal to be back in the

dingy little city office, where he planned his campaigns and enjoyed his triumphs. All the pleasure, you see, was in the anticipation.

This is often the case, also, in planning a holiday. For weeks beforehand you spend long hours in poring over guide-books, studying time-tables, working out routes, and interviewing tourist agents. What a time you are going to enjoy! And when the tour begins, you wonder what you left home for. Was it to see this? Is that the paradise pictured in the guide-books and praised in the rail-way advertisements? It is grand, cer-tainly; but you expected so much more. All the pleasure was in the anticipation. So when you visit a great man, you look fowrard with eager delight to the match-less wit and the lofty wisdom you will gain from his lips. And when the inter-view is over, you are asking to what accident that man owes his reputation.

He was positively dull; and yet the
world hangs upon his utterances.

Superficial as pleasure is, it occupies a
very large and prominent part in life.
Men will do for pleasure what nothing
else under heaven could prevail upon
them to attempt. See the athletic young
men grinding their bicycles up a steep hill
till the machines groan under the desperate and painful effort. If requested by
their employers to work with half this
zeal and persistence, they would promatly
and indignantly resign. See the dense
swaying mass of people outside a theatre,
clamoring for admission. They will endure the utmost inconvenience and dis-
comfort in order to obtain a few hours
of recreation. The love of pleasure in-
fluences the masses with magnetic effect.
It is hardly an exaggeration to say that
the man who writes a popular song exerts
a greater power than the man who pro-
duces a thousand sermons. The most

brilliant discourse will only reach a few thousand hearers; and even when the press gives it wings, and sends it fluttering through ten thousand homes, its work is still limited. But think of the immeasurable power of song. A million sermons would not reach the people who have been influenced by the " Lost Chord" or the "Better Land."

It is time that the Church took her part in providing rational pleasures for the people. Why not start a music-hall and run it on right lines, without beer and without vulgarity? Why should Christianity calmly submit to be outdone in this direction? With certain classes the Church has absolutely no chance. Its doors are opened on fifty days in the year, but the theatres and the music halls are busy for three hundred days in the year, and it is not difficult for the devil to outdo in six nights the good which the Church has accomplished in one. We want some one to do for the people's amusements what the London Religious Tract Society, and many private firms have done for the people's literature. In one case the argument is this: " Here are bad books that stir up evil passions, disseminate degrading thoughts, and work the ruin of the people. Now books are not in themselves bad. Let us therefore provide good reading, that shall be as interesting and attractive as the bad; reading that shall be pure but not puritanical, mildly exciting but not contaminating and scrofulous." Why should we not reason in the same eminently wise and practical way regarding amusements ? Let us argue thus : " Here is a great city, absolutely honeycombed with places of amusement. Some of them are hopelessly bad and demoralizing, the atmosphere is fœtid and enervating, and the entertainment is often unblushingly filthy. And yet amusement is not necessarily an evil. It has been shown that there is a profitable market for good books. Why not also as large a demand for pure pleasures? Let us therefore provide laughter that shall be clean, merriment that shall have no pain in it, pleasure that shall never be the forerunner of torment." The wise and Christian policy is to support and promote the good, and to reject and annihilate the evil. Pure amusements would do as much to promote the welfare of the people as high-class fiction has done.

I cannot imagine any man finding satisfactory delight in dancing. There may be no harm in a quiet dance amongst the home circle. But the public dancing-rooms are nothing less than dens of destruction. Dancing, when indulged in at promiscuous assemblies, has two grave dangers. There is a tendency to make it the one business of life; indeed, I have known men whose conversation seldom

rose beyond vague and mysterious discussions regarding the relative value of
the waltz and schottisch. It also leads to
late hours, and you may be quite sure that
the young man who turns up at business
in evening dress, with sleepy eyes, weary
frame, and a splitting headache, will soon
find himself presented with an indefinite
holiday. Dancing has been described as
" hugging to music, " and it is undoubtedly true that, apart from the music, Mrs.
Grundy would soon step in and put a stop
to the whole business. It is said that
dancing leads to marriage. That may be
true ; but who would care to look for a
wife amongst the giddy, thoughtless,
gushing creatures at a public dance ?

Pleasure is an excellent thing if it is
well chosen, wisely guarded and vigor-
ously controlled. So long as you can
master it and keep it in its place, all will
be well ; but give yourself up to it, and
the Biblical prophecy shall be fulfilled,

" He that loveth pleasure shall be a poor man." The most pleasureless man in the world is the man whose whole life is devoted to the pursuit of pleasure. Pleasure is like fire—a useful and indispensable servant, but a dangerous and fatal master. A room with a fire in it is comfortable ; a room all fire means death and destruction. So it is with pleasure. A life with pleasure in it is entirely right and satisfactory ; but a life all pleasure is not life at all, the grand purposes of life are forgotten, the noblest ideals are buried under a load of reckless mirth and senseless tomfoolery.

I am not speaking rashly, but with careful forethought, and as the result of some years of observation and experience, when I say that the cause of failure in five out of every six young men is the insane passion for pleasure. Thousands of men come to the large cities every year, all bent upon success. What is the result?

Their great aims are soon forgotten, their youthly enthusiasm quickly cools, and they have to rub along with a small wage which hardly keeps them alive. The cause is not always to be found in lack of ability or failure of character. It lies in a love of debilitating and unwholesome pleasures. When they should be engaged in healthful physical exercises or in strenuous mental improvement, they are kicking up their heels in a dancing-hall, or stewing in the gallery of a third-rate theatre. Such men will fail, inevitably and completely. They will sink by degrees. Gambling will fascinate them, strong drink will stupefy them, bad men will victimise them, and through love of pleasure they will become "poor men," stunted in intellect, enfeebled in body, ruined in soul.

Beware, then, my brothers, of riotous and irrational pleasures. The disillusionment is swift and terrible, and leaves a lasting scar behind. The pleasures that satisfy and invigorate are to be found in sturdy exercise, in healthful rambles through the verdant country, or amid the exquisite and ever-varying delights of the sea-shore, in the enjoyment of good books, noble pictures, and soul-stirring music. These are pleasures upon which you can ask the blessing of God, pleasures in which you can look for the companionship of your Master, Christ. They may not *excite*, but they *recreate*, and that is what you want. Remember, no man has a right to any enjoyment until he has earned it by steady, persevering toil. Before you can properly appreciate an evening's pleasure, you must do a day's work, and do it with thoroughness and alacrity. Those who never do any work never enjoy a holiday.

Remember, also—and this is the chief thing after all—that the truest pleasure to be found on earth is in self-sacrificing, Christian service. The only happy life is that which is lived "unto God." Spend much of your leisure in trying to bring heaven's rest nearer to earth's weariness. Succour the helpless, stand up for the oppressed, oppose every prevailing evil, seek the highest welfare of men, and you will experience a sacred rapture in the glowing brightness of which all earth's superficial pleasures will rapidly fade away. Such work will prevent all morbid introspection, all the wretched *ennui* of a self-centred existence, and it will drive away all melancholy and gloom. The only lasting pleasure is that which is found in an inflexible allegiance to duty, and in earnest social service for Jesus Christ.

V.

CHRIST AND COMMERCE.

" O, while you live, tell truth, and shame the devil."
—SHAKESPEARE.

IF there is anything which Christianity needs to-day it is the practical and sagacious help of business men. Christianity has suffered more from the dense stupidity of some of its followers than from the venomous opposition of all its enemies. A lazy, half-hearted, careless Christian can do more harm to Christ's cause than the most unscrupulous atheist. And if there is anything which commerce needs to-day, it is the cleansing ennobling influence of Christianity. The men who are immersed in the burning excitement and relentless whirl of business will be almost surprised if you tell them that Christianity is of far greater importance than all their commerce. They will laugh with a scornful incredulity, but it is a simple fact nevertheless. And for this reason, that commerce builds a fortune, but Christianity builds a character; commerce gives you a bank balance, but Christianity gives you an unfailing fund of happiness; commerce makes money, but Christianity makes men. And it makes what Carlyle used to call, "upright, downright, straightforward, all-round men." It smashes the unjust weights, breaks in pieces the fraudulent measures, banishes all trickery and cunning, kills the ready and plausible lie, and enables weak, imperfect, tempted men to practice the highest truthfulness and the sturdiest honesty.

I fear it must be admitted that these are days of great commercial corruption. There is, for instance, a despiciable system of bribery which is cleverly and conveniently disguised by such terms as " commissions " and " presents." It is time that all this trickery should be abolished, so that the polished rogues who have for so long waxed fat on the " usual commission," may be compelled to give up their secret spoils and enjoy the refreshing novelty of honest work. Then there is the scandalous and revolting system of "sweating," and many other foul systems of oppression and injustice, which indicate that the commercial atmosphere sadly needs the purifying influence of a living Christianity.

The Churches have been greatly to blame for much of the anti-Christian character of present-day commerce. They have busied themselves with theological sham-fights, and have played at conflicts in the clouds, when they ought to have descended into the actual throbbing, palpitating life of the people and fought a stern battle for uprightness and rectitude. And they have smilingly and gratefully accepted the haughty patronage and substantial checks of their wealthy supporters, without a single inquiry as to the glaring immoralities by which these men had heaped up their ill-gotten spoils. Henceforth the battle of Christianity will, to a large extent, have to be fought out in the counting-house and the ware-house. And the victory will not have been won so long as it is possible for men to be received with ringing cheers in religious assemblies, while they are grinding the life out of their unhappy employes, and indulging in practices which may be regarded in the city as commercially expedient, but looked at in the light of Christ's gospel are absolutely antagonistic to truth and righteousness.

There is one lie which needs to be promptly and publicly exposed. I refer to the miserable delusion which supposes that a man cannot be at once honest and successful in business. The best answer to this debasing theory is to be found in the lives of such men as the late William

E. Dodge, of New York, and Samuel
Morley, of London. They were as un-
swervingly upright as they were enor-
mously prosperous. It is an undeniable
fact that the principles of the sermon on
the Mount, when faithfully carried out,
form the surest guide to genuine success
in the market-place of to-day. The man
who gains a reputation for scrupulous
fidelity is the man everybody will want
to do business with. Let him guard the
most trivial details of his business with
tender jealously, let him discharge every
obligation with rigorous exactness, and
then when success crowns his efforts, he
will have maintained what is worth far
more than countless fortunes, an un-
stained name, an unsullied record, and a
conscience void of offence.

"But," says a young man, "I have
been honest, but I have not been successful." Of course not! Merely negative
virtues are absolutely valueless. The

office boy is not promoted because he never stole the stamps, but on account of his energy and vigilance, his ability and intelligence. The post assigned to you now may seem woefully small and unimportant, but it is just the way in which you do or neglect these apparently trifling duties that will make or mar your future. Never be discouraged because your present position is humble and obscure. If you sit down and mourn you will never get on. Do you want a better place? Then *outgrow the one you are in.* Do your present work—lowly and monotonous as it may seem—with as much vigor and care as if it were of crowning importance. Fit yourself by strenuous culture for the opportunity which will surely come. But never dream that you can be a success because you abstain from downright evil. You have got to *do something*, and what is more, you have got to do it well, do it better than you have ever done it before, and do it better than any-body else can do it. Then success is sure to follow.

Do you think that business life is hum-drum and prosaic? That shows how little you know about it. I tell you it is full of sublimest romance and deepest in-terest. You may look back longingly to the days when men could make a valiant stand for the right, and prove their faith-fulness to God by going manfully to the stake. But circumstances make no differ-ence to the true hero. If you cannot fight the battle of purity and virtue in a city office, you would never have braved the faggot-fire in the old days of martyr-dom. There is a holy war to be waged to-day. Never were self-sacrificing, hero-ic young men so greatly needed as they are now. You have to preserve your own manhood chaste and pure in the midst of flaring enticements to evil. You have to promote a nobler spirit in commerce, a

more brotherly and righteous spirit, which
shall lift business into a sweeter atmosphere and turn the factory into a sanctu-
ary. Never believe that business is a
dull, bald, grey, uninteresting thing. It
simply glows with poetry and romance.
Let us peep into a little city office.
There is a young man, with a pale and
haggard countenance ; he sits on a high
stool counting checks. He earns barely
two dollars a day, and yet a year or two
ago he had the temerity to marry a fair,
sweet girl. He loved her, and laughed at
the warnings of stern, logical, social econ-
omists. Now, she is thin and weak and
ill ; and as he left her bedside this morn-
ing the doctor remarked in commanding
tones, that wine—" port, sir, good port "
—was absolutely necessary, and that a
change of air would soon be advisable.
And on twelve dollars a week ! A fifty
dollar bill is in the young man's hand.
How he trembles ! Dare he do it ?

Three months hence the amount can be repaid and no one will be the wiser. It is just the amount he needed! Oh, the desperate conflict; but he is gloriously victorious. He jumps from his stool, defies the tempting devil, locks the money in the safe, and whispers, in a voice broken with tears, "*Lord, help me!*"

Ah! the race of heroes is not extinct. There is plenty of romance in the apparently dull routine of business life. Men who toil cheerily and live celibate lives in order to care for a dear old mother who has no other helper; great-hearted fellows who might rise to wealth if they would stoop to trickery, but who keep their hands clean and their hearts pure in spite of all the chicanery and cunning of the city—these are earth's truest heroes. And you can do the same if you put your trust in the unfailing help of a living Christ.

Beware of mere *cleverness*. There is a superficial kind of shrewdness which is extremely dangerous. The man who is *only* clever is always in peril of becoming a trickster—ever dodging, shifting, and deceiving. In these days of shallow knowledge and empty boasting, men need to be restrained and guided by the great example of the Christ life. In the Master we have all the best qualities of the ideal manhood combined in a perfect model. He had a mind quick to perceive, and a soul pure and clear as the noonday sun. It is for this lofty character that we must strive and pray. We want intellectual alacrity, but we also want unflinching rectitude. "There is only one post for you," said Carlyle to a bad man, "and that is—perpetual president of the Heaven and Hell Amalgamation Society." There are many men in commerce of whom that would be true. They are engaged in a hopeless attempt to serve God and mammon—to increase their wealth by the maximum of swindling, while they try to deaden their conscience by the minimum of empty and formal pietism. It will never do. The attempt can only end in failure and dishonor and endless shame. But the man who by the power of an ever-present Christ has been able to conquer himself, who has calmly ignored the sneers of the cynic and resolutely withstood the wiles of the tempter—that man has in his heart the sublime consciousness of having done right, and his path is bathed in brightness. He is governed by principle instead of passion, by truth instead of trickery. His soul is possessed by an unspeakable peace, his heart is filled with an unfaltering trust in God, and he has no damning recollection of cruel wrong or foul injustice to darken his outlook and destroy his rest. He may not be followed by the fawning adulation of men, but with the pure in heart he will see God. And that will be far better than if he had gained the whole world and lost his own soul.

VI.

ABOUT HOLIDAYS.

If thou art worn and hard beset
With troubles that you wouldst forget,
If thou wouldst read a lesson that will keep
Thy heart from fainting and thy soul from sleep,
Go to the woods and hills! no tears
Dim the sweet look that Nature wears.

H. W. LONGFELLOW.

I BELIEVE no one in this world enjoys a holiday more thoroughly than the hard-working business young man, and for this reason—that fifty weeks of honest toil form the best possible preparation for two weeks' recreation. Many a man does not think so, I admit. When he sees the " gilded youths " who have nothing to do from January 1st to December 31st but go a-pleasuring, he looks around at his dingy office, counts the weary weeks that have to elapse before his humble two weeks' vacation, and feels like breaking the tenth commandment. He is under an immense delusion. "If all the year were playing holidays, to sport would be as tedious as to work." No man revels in twelve or twenty days' exemption from toil like the busy worker who has been plodding manfully for eleven long months to earn his bread, and who, in spare hours, has lived earnestly and fought valiantly in order to acquire a cultured mind and achieve a lofty character.

No man need forswear the luxury of a holiday because he is poor. The most rational and refreshing delights are generally the cheapest. I have had better holidays for twenty dollars than I have had for two hundred. Those who travel most sometimes see the least. You may rush through Europe and squander your substance at fashionable hotels only to be bored by the inanity of *table-d'hote* chatter, bewildered by the eccentricities of railway porters, pestered by garrulous guides, and broiled by the hot suns of Continental cities. I shall never forget the fatigue I endured after my first visit to Paris. Those brilliant boulevards and glittering cafes and feverish crowds—how I tired of them all ; and how supremely happy I felt for a week afterwards, resting in a quiet French seaside town, where I could dine when I liked, dress as I liked, and do what I liked, and where no one thought it undignified to lie on the sands in flannels with the Tauchnitz edition of the last new romance. I would not underrate the value of a European trip to a healthy young man—nothing surely could be more interesting or delightful ; but for a jaded mind and a weary body there is, perhaps, better relaxation to be found nearer home. There is no lack of variety in temperature and scenery within the compass of reasonable distance, and many delightful resorts are to be discovered by a little effort and inquiry.

When Mr. Ruskin urges us to play wisely as well as to work well, he gives us a very necessary and important advice. What can be more irrational than the way in which many people spend their holidays ? They frequently toil much harder during what they playfully term their " vacation " than under the most strenuous pressure of business. They either rush from monument to museum, from park to picture-gallery, from cafe to cathedral, in a cruel but conscientious attempt to "do Europe," or else they " rest " amid the shrill and vulgar choruses of nigger minstrels and the mad whirl of fashionable folly. All this is a huge blunder. Do you follow a sedentary occupation ? Then, why not spend your holiday on a wheel ? Mounted on a good cycle you can roam through the most charming country entirely at your own sweet will. The expense is inconsiderable, the exercise healthy, and the enjoyment boundless. Others will prefer rowing, and will gain equally beneficial results. I always feel that the vain creatures who deck themselves in gorgeous raiment, squander money on unnecessary luxuries, and then start up and down the crowded promenade of a fashionable resort all day, and breathe the vitiated atmosphere of the dancing saloon at night, are greatly to be pitied. What do they know of the simple, honest pleasures of pure air, plain food, genial companionship, and healthy exercise? Yet these are the chief desiderata of a real holiday, and while their value is priceless their cost is insignificant.

How can we make sure of an exhilarating and thoroughly satisfactory holiday? Let me offer a few friendly suggestions. (1.) *By going at the right time.* September is probably the best month, if you can conveniently manage it. The air is cool and bracing, popular resorts are not

overcrowded, and the voice of the stroll-
ing musician is no longer heard in the
streets. (2.) *By earning it.* The man
who has worked perseveringly throughout the year goes away with a clear conscience, and enjoys his vacation with a
buoyancy of spirit and a lightness of
heart sufficient to turn the idler and
lounger green with envy. (3.) *By pre-
paring for it.* The joys of anticipation
are often greater than the pleasures of
realization. Having chosen a place that
will suit your tastes and temperament,
read up all the best books that refer to it,
plan a pleasant route, and inquire for
comfortable but not necessarily expen-
sive quarters. (4.) *By sharing it with
genial companions.* It is far better to
be alone than to endure the endless
cackle of feather-brained chatterers, or
the morbid growls of dyspeptic cynics.
Amongst "genial companions " I would
include books. To enjoy a holiday we

need not put aside all work. What we want, as a rule, is not so much entire rest as change of scene and occupation. Why not take a few books for which no time could be found in the work-days ? To read *about* the places visited will help to store the mind with useful information. (5.) *By keeping your eyes wide open.* I know men who have been veritable globe-trotters, and yet they are as insular in their sympathies, and as narrow in their information, as the most thorough-bred Cockney. All the inspiring paint-ings and noble architecture, all the pre-cious memorials of genius and antiquity, have failed to make the slightest impres-sion ; but they will tell you with the ut-most gravity, that in London the cost of shaving was only half as much as in New York; that in Venice the lodgings were shockingly vile ; and that Paris was the only place where they could get decent coffee.

Holidays have their dangers. Restraints are removed—no one knows you —and you are in the extremely perilous position of being able to do as you like. I have seen young men do things abroad which they would have solemnly condemned at home. Beware of the "gaiety of those whose headaches nail them to a noonday bed; whose haggard eyes flash desperation and betray pangs." Healthy merriment and innocent pleasure will do us all good; but may God save us from the "gaiety that fills the bones with pain, the mouth with blasphemy, and the heart with woe." There is such a gaiety, and it flashes with seductive charm in many a holiday haunt. No recreation is worth the name which does not make us buoyant with renewed health, eager for social service, and strong for daily toil.

VII.

SHAMS.

"Some that smile have in their hearts, I fear, millions of mischiefs."—SHAKESPEARE.

"You can fool some of the people all the time, and all the people some of the time, but you can't fool all the people all the time."—ABRAHAM LINCOLN.

To say that a sham is the most despicable thing in the world is merely to utter an obvious truism. To observe that society is cursed by shams is only to express the most general sentiment. And yet it is possible that we have not altogether realized how deplorable is the influence of the hypocritical spirit—how it poisons the moral atmosphere, hinders all good work, and casts a withering blight over everything it touches. The weakest point in any body of men is that occupied by the counterfeits, the frauds, the impostors. Any political party might attain office to-morrow if all its followers were

downright in earnest. Christianity might
conquer the world in a year if every man
who bears the name of Christ were determined, loyal, burning with fervid zeal,
and thoroughly genuine and sincere.
Then every disciple would be terrible in
battle, irresistible in prayer, and stalwart
in faith. But the victory is postponed by
the half-hearted, the hesitating, the shams,
the hypocrites, the people who are never
to be depended upon.

Let us glance rapidly at a few of these
counterfeits. Perhaps the most terrible
hindrance to the free and unrestricted
progress of Christianity is the *religious
sham*. The question that proves such a
stumbling-block to thousands of intelli-
gent and large-hearted young men to-day
is this: "How is it that while professing Christians are frequently mean and
selfish and proud, worldlings are so often
generous and brotherly and Christ-like?"
"Look there," said a young man to Pro-

fessor Drummond, " you see that elderly
gentleman ? He is the founder of our infidel club." " But, " said the Professor,
" he is a leading elder of the Church."
" I know he is, " was the young man's
reply, " but he founded our infidel club.
Every man in the village knows what a
humbug he is, and so we will have nothing to do with religion." It is all very
well to say that Christianity should not be
judged by such feeble and unworthy spec-
imens—the fact remains that it is judged
by those who profess it ; and so long as
that is the case, every sham representa-
tive will be a source of weakness and a
hindrance to all true progress.

The religion which is going to influence
the world to-day is a religion not merely
of creeds but of conduct—a religion that
softens the heart, controls the passions,
checks the hasty and impatient word, and
purifies the life both of the home and the
office. " I would not give much for that

man's religion," said Rowland Hill, "whose very cat and dog are not better for it." Every Christian should so live as to be able to say with the good old Methodist preacher, "If you don't believe I am a Christian, ask my wife!" A religion which is confined to a prayer-meeting is a counterfeit religion, and may be swept away as absolutely valueless; true Christianity sweetens the whole life, and uplifts everything it touches. There is no better defense of Christianity than the generous character and upright life of a true man, and there is no more dangerous enemy of Christianity than the creature who steals "the livery of the Court of Heaven to serve the devil in," whose tongue is fluent with plausible professions while his hands are busy with the works of hell.

An Athenian once delivered a long and brilliant speech, in which he made large and liberal promises. Another—who

lacked eloquence but was full of sincerity
—got up and said, "Men of Athens, all
that he has *promised* I will *do.*" That
is the spirit we need to-day. There is
nothing more pitiable than to see good
men wasting time and talent in little,
unworthy squabbles about their pet dog-
mas, while their next door neighbors are
going to the devil for want of a strong
arm of help and a kindly word of cheer.
The man who boasts that his soul is
saved and never feeds a poor body or
cheers a sad heart is a living contradic-
tion—an awful sham! "Quit your meanness" is a favorite expression with a certain revival preacher, and really it is a
very necessary piece of advice. The
popular idea of religion is a comfortable,
jog-trot, respectable kind of life—an oc-
casional visit to a church, a prompt pay-
ment of pew rents, a few stray sub-
scriptions to painfully importunate collec-

tors, and then you may be as selfish and cynical as the rest of the world. This is meanness—contemptible and pitiable. We can do without these lazy sentiment-alists. these *dilettanti* church-goers, these religious shams, who never do a day's helpful work to relieve the world's agony or minister to the world's necessi-ties. There are thousands of young men in our homes and churches who indo-lently stand aloof from the great battle for good and right and truth. Is this manly. or chivalrous, or Christ-like? Is it not cowardly and selfish and mean? How can we be surprised if the Master should pronounce over all such shams those sad words that are full of tears. " Inasmuch as ye did it not——"

Then there is the sham in *business*. He is lazy. flabby, slovenly, careless. He shrinks from the monotony of routine, despises the daily drudgery, postpones every disagreeable duty, and then wonders how it is that he is such an utter failure in life. Lowell has told us that

Folks thet worked thorough was the folks that thriv,
But bad work follers ye ez long's ye live,
Ye can't get red on't just az sure az sin,
It's allers askin' to be done agin.

We all know men who work in this superficial way: They do everything lazily, partially, unsatisfactorily. Their work will not bear inspection—it may be showy, but it is also valueless. What thou doest, do *well*, is the best motto for young men to-day. The man who knows how to do one thing thoroughly, and is determined to do it better than anybody else, is the man who will succeed. Mr. Vanderbilt paid his cook a salary of $10,000 a year because he understood the art of cooking to perfection. As a well known humorist says in his funny way, "If Monsieur Sauceagravi could cook tolerably well, and shoot a little, and speak three languages tolerably well, and keep books fairly, and could telegraph a little—and so on with a dozen other things—he wouldn't get ten thousand a year for it." No, what is needed is strenuous concentration of effort. Aim definitely at one great object and bring all your powers to bear upon the work in hand, and you cannot fail to rise to fairer heights of honor and achievement.

Do you know the sham *sceptic*—the man who is glad of any excuse for trampling on Christianity? "I hate cant," he says, with great unction and self-satisfaction, forgetting that Christianity by no means possesses the monopoly in cant. There is a good deal of cant about some atheists. It is not always the "fool" who says "there is no God;" it is very frequently the arrogant sham, who thinks it supremely clever to display his shallow and flippant atheism. He will learn one day that honest, manly Christianity is

the avowed enemy of "cant," and hates
and suppresses it wherever it lurks,
whether in the form of superficial pietism
or hypocritical infidelity.

While I sympathize from my very
heart with earnest men who reject Christianity, because of the shortcomings of its
professors, I must still maintain that their
position is utterly childish and illogical.
It is really a most lamentable fact when
men come into the region of religion
they so often leave their common sense
behind them. In politics they are influenced by the great party leaders, not by
flabby wire-pullers. Sensible citizens do
not reject the Republican party when a
few weak-kneed constituents turn trai-
tors ; nor do honest Democrats falter at
the sight of a handful of feeble renegades.
And yet in religion the same persons will
allow their minds to be prejudiced by the
apparent inconsistencies of any blatant
professor, rather than go straight to

the great Founder of the Christian faith, who alone can show them what Christianity really is.   Surely the answer of Christ to any young man who excused himself from discipleship on account of the unlovely lives of professors, would be, " What is that to thee ?   *Follow thou Me.*"   It is neither fair nor manly to point to the failings of professing Christians as a reason for ignoring Jesus Christ. One man hunts up a bigot, another discovers a Pharisee, and a third glances sneeringly at some faltering and unhappy struggler who has blundered back into sin and shame ; and then in scornful chorus they cry, " Behold, this is Christianity !"   The derision is utterly unjust. Christ calls men to *Himself.* He is the typical man—His was the perfect life— He is the supreme example.

With every desire to look on the bright side of things and magnify the redeeming features of the age, I must frankly admit

that there is amongst men to-day a start-
ling amount of shallowness and superfici-
ality of thought. Instead of honestly
thinking out great problems, and labor-
iously unwinding the puzzles of life, they
indulge in mental gymnastics and hastily
jump at conclusions. We have all around
us feeble imitations of Robert Elsmere.
Such men meet a free-thinking friend,
listen to his tall but trumpery talk, and
immediately, with scarcely a moment's
heartache or an hour's mental struggle,
throw overboard the little religion they
possessed, and denounce the Evangel of
Christ as a myth and a sham. The most
uncertain of political weathercocks would
refuse to budge an inch on the flimsy
evidence which sends these young men
into the dreary night of a Christless life.
Can anything be more painful than the
careless and frivolous spirit with which
they leap into the cold abyss ? Self-con-
fident youths, with more collar than cul-

ture, and more millinery than manliness, swallow two or three pages of a magizine article, and, without questioning the credentials of the writer, calmly turn their back upon their Father God, and go out to sip the latest fashionable mixed drink at the hotel bar.

Very few of us have ever thought what it is to be a Christian. When we see a man ticketed as orthodox in creed and regular in church attendance, and then discover that he is harsh and bitter and sensual, we immediately begin to throw stones at Christianity. But that man is not a Christian! He may cry, "Lord, Lord," but loud professions will never open the kingdom of heaven. "Follow thou Me" is the great command. By no other test are we at liberty to judge our brethren. If any man lives the Christ life then he is a Christian, whatever may be the opinion of the pedantic critic or the priestly ceremonialist. The duty of every young man is not to dissect disciples but to study Christ. Pure religion and undefiled is to do the will of God on earth as angels do it in heaven.

Now turn for a moment to another kind of sham—the society sham—the miserable spirit of counterfeit respectability. It is not greatly afraid of evil, but it particularly hates the *appearance* of evil. "People might talk"—that is the awful bogie that frightens society, and the characterless chatter of brainless men and women is more to be dreaded than all the bitterness of wrongdoing. This hypocritical system of sham respectability is dead against those peculiar "people" who hold out hands of welcome and friendship to ragged castaways, prodigals, and sinners, and do other strange and eccentric things. It crushes kindliness out of young hearts; smothers the vivacity of buoyant spirits; reckons decorum to be more than purity, good breeding to be far above honesty, and the esteem of Society (with a large " s ") to be infinitely preferable to Heaven's " Well done ! " You may be mean, selfish, and cowardly ; but you must not eat peas with your knife. You may be hard-hearted, cynical, and cruel, if you will, but consent to wear an unhealthy and uncomfortable stove-pipe hat on Sundays, and avoid speaking to any man to whom you have not been formally introduced. It has a smile for the well-dressed *debauche*, the polite and wealthy knave ; but it would cast into outer darkness the repentant Magdalene to whom Christ extended infinite sympathy.

Beware of this cold, critical, carping spirit. Beware of the slavery of society, the thraldom of caste, the oppressive tyranny of custom. Think for yourselves, use the intellect with which God has blessed you, and prove yourselves the *conquerers*, not the *creatures*, of circumstances. Goodness is the truest nobility. The man who has faith in God, love for humanity, and the resolve to live a Christ-like life, can afford to ignore all the threatenings of social ostracism, and wait patiently till the brotherhood of men shall be universally acknowledged.

One of the most discouraging features of life amongst young men is the prevalence of *sham-cynicism.* A clever writer but short-viewed critic, who is a living example of this unhealthy habit, tells us in a recent article that "the young man of to-day has no religion and no enthusiasm," that he is ready to "throw a woman on the dissecting table," and that to him love is nothing but "a cruel enigma." Can anything be more utterly ridiculous? To mix with small-minded pessimists, listen to the unclean tittle-tattle of the club, and then rush into the awful belief that chivalry is dead, and that faith and earnestness no longer exist, is about as sane an action as that of the man who dissected a dust-heap and then denounced the world as a great conglomeration of putrid ashes. Thank God the great mass of young men are true in heart and upright in life. Melancholy cynics and *blase* club-men may not believe it, but there are thousands of men to-day who prefer to feed on Kingsley and Tennyson and Longfellow rather than pink sporting papers and cheap works of scandal—generous and high-minded men who can grapple with giant temptations and control the reins of passion, because they have grasped the hand of Christ and asked Him to keep them pure and strong. Let us beware of hastily judging the whole race of young men by the cheap cynicism of a few battered *roues*. "Continue for ever," said Carlyle, "to take the *best* view of all mortals which your understanding will admit; nay, it is often also truer than the surly one."

There are other shams, of which the merest mention is sufficient. There is the sham who is a smiling philanthropist in the church, and a frowning tyrant in his business. There is the sham who wins a woman's pure affection by his fair words, and then wrecks her young life by his foul animalism. There is the sham who eloquently advocates reform on the platform, while his own house is devoid of order or comfort. There is the sham who says there is no God, because it will be easier to lie and swindle when he has persuaded himself into that belief.

The only cure for shams is at the Cross. No counterfeit can live at Calvary. There the hypocrisy is pierced, the mask falls off, and all is revealed. But there also we find forgiveness, there all the wild and bitter past is blotted out; there we learn to love, there we begin to live.

VIII.

THE LOST CHRIST.

Abide in me !   There have been moments blest,
  When I have heard Thy voice and felt Thy power;
Then evil lost its grasp; and passion, hushed,
  Owned the divine enchantment of the hour.

These were but seasons, beautiful and rare:
  Abide in me and they shall ever be!
Fulfill at once Thy precept and my prayer:
  Come, and abide in me, and I in Thee!

—MRS. H. B. STOWE.

IN the second chapter of Luke there is a most significant and instructive incident. Jesus, a boy of twelve, had gone with His parents to Jerusalem to attend the Feast of the Passover. At the close of the great festival, Joseph and Mary joined their friends and set out for home ; but after a day's journey they discovered, to their bitter consternation, that they had come without Jesus. A simple, unexciting incident—but one that is pregnant with meaning, and one that conveys a

(102)

most helpful message to the young men of to-day.

They *"supposed* Him to have been in the company." That was their supreme mistake. Christ's presence is so essential that it must never become a matter of careless supposition or momentary speculation. There is more hope of the man who deliberately turns his back upon Christ, frankly confesses his entire disbelief of the Gospel, and cuts off all connection with the church, than of the weak, superficial, backboneless professor, who swallows his father's creed to save trouble, keeps what little religion he has as quiet and obscure as possible to avoid persecution, and then " supposes " it is all right. But "suppose" it is not all right, " suppose " Christ is not with you, " suppose " you are like a rudderless boat in a hurricane—impotent, feeble, demoralized—without guide or light or friend ? This is a matter about which we must be

definite and sure. Let everything else
go, but at least aim at the certitude and
safety which come of daily intercourse
with Christ, who alone can secure our
highest welfare, promote our most perfect
happiness, and cleanse our lives from corruption and sin.

Be careful that you do not lose Christ,
for His presence is the only guarantee of
a safe and joyous life. Mr. Quintin Hogg
tells a remarkable story of an incident
which happened at one of our largest
clubs. He was chatting with a friend
about a man who had died by his own
hand. His friend spoke rather indignantly of such an ignoble termination to life,
and characterized it, rightly enough, as a
cowardly thing for a man to leave others
to meet the troubles and reap the bitter
harvest he had sown. A well-known
scientific man, who was sitting close by,
turned round and said, " I think you have
expressed a very harsh judgment. I

don't consider it the action of a coward, and, for myself, the only rest I can look forward to is the grave." Mr. Hogg's friend, thinking that perhaps the gentleman had lost some dear relative by suicide, qualified his remarks by saying that such crimes were generally committed under the influence of a deranged mind, and that his words did not, of course, apply to a man who was irresponsible for his acts. "There is something worse than derangement," was the reply, "and that is despair." Mr. Hogg says that his friend was very much shocked at the words, and at the tone in which they were uttered, and began to speak to the scientist as best he could about the love of God. He told him that he could not imagine how those who accepted the help of God could ever despair. "Ah!" was the sad reply, "I gave up my belief in God long ago, and I have had nothing but a deepening despair

ever since.   I repeat that the grave is the
only rest I can hope for—-the only home
that remains to me. ''

Was there ever a sadder story ?   Here
is a noted man of science making the
humiliating confession that life has lost all
its brightness, that the outlook is irre-
deemably black, and that he is in the
depths of perpetual despair.   He ap-
proaches the grave without God and
without hope—with nothing but disap-
pointment and darkness and defeat.   This
is what comes of *losing Christ.*   We
have no longer the power to overcome ;
we are the sport of circumstances, and
gradually we drift on to the cruel, grim,
frowning rocks of helpless misery.   The
story is like a glaring signal, warning us
of the danger that lies ahead.   It bids us
keep close to the strong, tender Christ—
to walk in His footsteps, to try to
live His simple, unselfish life—the life
that may sometimes be hard and rough

and bleak, but is always full of unfailing
hope and undimmed love, and bright with
the undoubted promise of ultimate victory.

Where was it that Joseph and Mary
missed the boy Christ? Not in the quiet
secluded home at Nazareth. No; they
lost Him in the city. That is the concise
record of many a young man to-day. In
the old country home it was easy enough
to live the Christ-life; but when you are
pitchforked into the huge city, with all its
bewildering multitudes, its disenchanting
realism, its seductive snares, and its mad-
dening perplexities, then it is that you are
in danger of missing the presence of the
Master. When you leave Nazareth for
Jerusalem, then comes the battle. From
the plain, lonely, healthful life of the country you plunge into the enervating, arti-
ficial, and restless existence of the city,
and it will be almost a miracle if in this
complete change of environment you do

not to some extent, lose the conscious presence of Christ.

But what I want to point out to you is this, that unfavorable circumstances are to be conquered. The stern discipline will do you good. Now you are in the city you will require the moral invigoration of Christ's companionship more than ever. The very strenuousness of city life will help to make your Christianity more practical, more manly, and, shall I say, more serviceable. The satisfaction of selfish and conventional religiousness is no match for the spiritual conflicts of the city. You will have no time to waste in quarrelling about doctrinal differences or in arranging the complicated mechanism of creeds. You want a strong, virile Christianity, which does not frown on the beauties of art, nor fear the researches of science, nor shut its eyes to the charms of music, nor leave the gymnasium and outdoor sport to be the playthings of the devil. This is the Christianity which is to save the city, purging its pleasures and ennobling its thoughts and elevating every detail of its life. It says to young men who are sinking into the aimless existence of the worldling, or the cold, songless despair of the unbeliever, " Brother, you do not only want a Christ who is far away in the dim records of ancient history; you want a friendly arm to guide you and lift you up. The real Christ is a wise counsellor and a loving companion. He will not rob you of a single pleasure. He will not crush your inquiring spirit or dethrone your intellect. He will charm you by His tenderness, deliver you from the tyranny of passion, and enable you to do the will of God on earth." This is the Evangel for the field of sport, the Gospel for the counting-house, the salvation for the city, and, thank God, thousands of the city young men have listened to its message, and have joyfully received

Jesus Christ as a Friend and Brother and Savior. They love the Man of Nazareth—the Christ of God and the Savior of men—with an ardent and unspeakable affection which inevitably constrains them to toil for the welfare and happiness of their race. They live a large, free, happy life, and they live it supremely for that great Master whose presence is its sublime inspiration, and whose " Well done ! " is its highest reward

But I notice, also, that Christ was lost during the excitement of a feast, and many men to-day could testify that they have found His presence less real and their own love less warm, as the result of reckless indulgence or irrational pleasures. It was in a *crowd*, too, that Jesus was missed—and it is the busy whirl and riotous rush of modern life that endangers our unbroken communion with heaven. We live at a desperate pace, every hour is occupied by the bustle of business or the fever of amusement, and so in the jostling of the crowd it seems as if He had slipped away, and behold! the light of our life has gone out, we miss His smile and fear to take another step because we have lost His protection. Brothers, this must not be. We must have our quiet hours of seclusion and repose lest the world should altogether absorb our attention.

But there is a cheering sequel to the story of the lost Christ. They found Him. Directly they discovered that He was missing, they went back to Jerusalem to look for the lost Christ. But here is a fact which we must not ignore. It did not take one day to lose Christ, but it took three days to find Him. How true that is! A foul jest, an impure thought, an hour's dalliance with sin, and the sunshine of His presence is eclipsed. And then comes the long and bitter repentance that rends the heart, the weary soul-tormenting search for the deserted Lord. Let us not despair, however, for Christ was found in the city after all. Persevere manfully, hopefully—do not give up, even when the search seems to be in vain. Christ is never very far from those who seek Him, and even in the city—dark and bitter and unwholesome as it may be—He is to be found by honest hearts and true.

The end of the story points a useful moral for young men in great cities. They found Christ in the Temple, and you, my brother, will most likely find Him there too. Nothing is more distressing to ministers than to witness the small proportion of young men in our churches. Nothing is more spiritually suicidal than the way in which men neglect the house of prayer. One reason for this is ignorance. Many young men, who in other respects are sane and reasonable, have a most baseless and unworthy prejudice

against preachers. But no manly, honest
fellow will allow himself to be fettered by
prejudice. Seek for Christ, therefore,
in the Temple. In the calm, quiet sanc-
tuary some sweet song may cheer you ;
some noble utterance may inspire you;
and Christ Himself may enter your heart
and make it to throb with love—touch your
lips and set them on fire with a message
to the world, and clasp your hands and
make them busy in His service. Then
you will know the joy of faith and the
rapture of self-sacrifice. Then life will be
worth living.

And now as we finish the story of the
lost Christ, we may well ask : Is He
with us to-day, not only as a personal
friend and Savior, but as a powerful influence in the larger life of the nation ?
Is the spirit of Christ bringing us nearer
to the social regeneration of mankind ?
Looking out upon the world the first im-
pression is deeply discouraging. First of

all, there is a distressing overplus of laborers. Strong men, eager for honest toil, endure the agonies of hunger and exposure, and in many cases the additional sorrow of beholding the sufferings of their family. On the other hand, overwhelming wealth is often allied with avarice and immorality, and while the poor starve by inches, the rich—to a large extent—ignore the needs of their brethren, and are only solicitous that Lazarus should not become inconveniently prominent. Thousands of young men are forced to slave in cramped shops and cheerless warehouses for sixty and seventy hours a week, with never an interval for physical recreation or intellectual improvement. In attics and cellars women sew shirts or make cheap clothing for inhuman "sweaters" for a wage which is insufficient for the rent of a bed—not to speak of a separate room—and are often compelled to choose between starvation and vice. In other sections of the same cities whole streets are in the possession of rouged and painted sirens of sensuality and sin— every one a standing rebuke to the weakness and wickedness of man. Europe literally bristles with bayonets, and instead of settling trifling disputes by wise and fair consultation, the nations continue to rush into the mad devilry of carnage and conflagration. As for the young men, thousands of them are gambling themselves into prison, or drinking themselves into early graves ; and yet every respectable newspaper is occupied with long reports of horse-races, and a so called Christian Community permits a saloon to be planted at the corner of every street. Sin is made easy, vice is made cheap, trickery prevails in trade, bitterness in politics, and apathy in religion. Does not the glad message of " Peace on earth, goodwill to men," which the angels once rang out over the moonlit meadows

of Bethlehem, seem like a ghastly satire
in ears accustomed to the rumors of war
the strife of parties, and the cries of the
oppressed ?

Nevertheless, I maintain that Christ is
with us, and that there is a growing rec-
ognition of human brotherhood the world
over. Years ago we should have been
unmoved by the horror and iniquity of
war. The social sores which alarm and
distress us to-day would have been regarded as normal aud irredeemable. But
to the enlightened vision of earnest Christians they now appear diabolical and degrading, and this very fact proves that we
are advancing. Let those who think that
the general outlook is becoming more
dismal, read the history of what we ironi-
cally call the " good old times." They
will find that at a period within the memory of many now living, one-seventh of the
inhabitants of Liverpool, England, lived
in cellars, five-sixths of the inhabitants of

Rochdale had scarcely a blanket apiece, one person in every eleven throughout England was receiving relief from the poor rates, and three children out of four were receiving no schooling whatever. Children of six, five, or even four years of age, were kept at hard work in the mines, and hunger, disease, ignorance, and brutal vice were alarmingly prevalent. Of course, if it is any consolation to unhealthy pessimists to believe that we are inevitably getting worse, then who would deny them that tender and refreshing thought? But we may well rejoice in the fact that the general aspect of social life was never so bright as it is to-day. Poverty and impurity and intemperance still exist, but the way to fight and annihilate these evils is not to sit down and sigh, but to be up and doing with cheerful alacrity and tireless preseverance.

Surely it is a striking indication of the

presence of Christ and the vitality of Christianity when great evils are regarded as intolerable. If our hearts are saddened by the awful contrast between grim poverty and glittering wealth, we may find hope and courage in the fact that real, vigorous, common-sense Christianity is making unmistakable progress. The day of hollow shams, of rigid formalism and luxurious selfishness, is nearly over. Thank God, all Christians are not lounging in cushioned pews and comforting one another with the assurance that

> Doing is a deadly thing ;
> Doing ends in death.

Some have discovered that to contemplate the prospective glories of heaven is not nearly so useful as to bring heaven's glory down to earth. The genius of true religion is practical beneficence, and it cannot be deaf to the cry of human sorrow and need ; it must take the great bleeding world to its heart, and tend it lovingly until all its wounds are healed.

Let us be of good cheer, for Christ is not lost. We know He is with us, for we see an ever-increasing spirit of brother-hood extending throughout the world. We know He is with us, for there is springing up a self-sacrificing burden-bearing, truth-loving Christianity, which shall yet dispel the appalling gloom of earth's despair. Christ Himself is with us, and He is calling upon every young man to join in the bloodless battle for righteousness. Be silent and stagnant and selfish no longer. Give Him your unwavering trust, your unquestioning obedience, your undivided love, and in return He will give you a life that shall be joyous, serene, triumphant.

www.ingramcontent.com/pod-product-compliance
Lightning Source LLC
Chambersburg PA
CBHW032012010726
47493CB00007B/2374